THE BUSINESS PRESENTER'S POCKETBOOK

ROSSIE SCHOOL
MONTROSE
ANGUS DD10 9TW

By John Townsend *5th Edition*

"Part of every Team Training Manager's presentation kit" - Dr Hubert König, Managing Director, Team Training, Austria.

"Excellent reference point for all managers who have to make presentations" - Keith Allen, Vice President Human Resources (Europe, Middle East and Africa) with Northern Telecom.

CONTENTS

Page

1. Organizing your Presentation (Murphy's Law, The 3 W's - Why, What, Who ?, Structure, Notes)   1

2 .Making your Presentation (The Bangs, Nerves, Voice, Dress, Platform Skills, Eyes, Timing, Mannerisms, Discussion Leading, Dealing with Questions/Difficult Participants, Golden Rules)   9

3. Audio-Visual Aids (The Flip-Chart, The Overhead Projector, The Slide Projector, The Cassette Recorder, VHF Communication)   27

4. Presentation Checklist (A way to beat Murphy's Law)   63

CHECKLIST

5. Television Interviews (What you say, How you say it, How to answer questions)   67

6. Press Conferences (Gaining time, Gaining empathy, Gaining Control)   77

7. Feedback (How to give and receive constructive critique)   85

FEEDBACK

8. Masters for Reproduction (Notes card, Checklist, Feedback Card)   89

MASTERS

1. ORGANIZING YOUR PRESENTATION

ORGANIZING YOUR PRESENTATION
MURPHY'S LAW

> **If something can go wrong - it will !**

The only way to beat Murphy's Law of Business Presentations is with the **3 P's:**

- **Preparation**
- **Preparation**
- **Preparation**

O'Connor's Corollary
Murphy was an Optimist !

ORGANIZING YOUR PRESENTATION
THE 3 W's

WHY ?

"A wise man asks himself seven times 'why?' before acting"

- Why am I going to give this presentation ?
  - To provide information? • To represent my function?
  - To entertain? • To fill up the agenda? • To sell my ideas?
  - To defend a position? • To be provocative?
- Whatever the answer, keep asking 'why?' in other ways...............
  - What is the objective I wish to achieve?
  - What is happening **now** that I wish to change or clarify?
  - What will I accept as evidence that my speech has succeeded?
  - What must the audience do or think at the end?
  ......until it becomes obvious **WHAT** your essential messages must be

(3)

THE 3 W's

WHAT ?

- ● Answering the question 'why?' properly will tell you **what** your main messages should be. But, however intelligent your audience is, they will neither want nor be able to absorb more than:
  - • **4 or 5 Keypoints**

- ● Since you have a lot of competition for other speakers (and television !) you need a **VEHICLE** to carry your message to the audience. After all, if your presentation is not memorable - why bother to speak ? Good vehicles include:
  - • **A mnemonic device** to link key messages together and help retention (an example is 'Bomber B' on Page 6)
  - • **An analogy, parable or example** to make a bridge between your messages and the audience's experience.
  - • **A series of slides** to "package" your messages

THE 3 W's

WHO ?

Once you know exactly **why** you are going to make the presentation and **what** your key points will be, you must ask **who will be in the audience ?** - so as to customise your message and make it stick.

- Who are the participants ? Level ? Background ?
- What do they already know about the subject ?
- Are they really interested ? (If not, I'll have to create the interest)
- What are their W.I.F.M's ?! (**W**hat's **I**n it **F**or **M**e ?)
- How fast can they absorb what I'm saying ?
- What do they **expect** me to say ?
- What is their mind-set ? (prejudices, attitudes, beliefs etc.)

To be sure you have tailored your speech to the audience, play devil's advocate and ask " how could I best offend them if I really wanted to ?!"

(5)

ORGANIZING YOUR PRESENTATION
STRUCTURE
"BOMBER B"
A mnemonic device to help you structure your presentation and make it fly !

Bang !
- Always start with an attention-getting "hook"

Opening
- Outline main messages (Road Map)

Message
- Give only 4-5 key messages

Bridge
- Make a bridge between each key message and the participant's experience and needs (WIFM's)

Examples
- Give frequent examples to help the audience visualize what you mean

Recap
- Be sure to summarize and conclude

Bang !
- Always finish with a closing "hook"

Readers of "The Instructor's Pocketbook" will recognize Bomber B as the nickname of B. Gunar Edeg R.A.F.(B) the Icelandic pilot who helps trainers to stucture their courses !

Business Presentations

ORGANIZING YOUR PRESENTATION
NOTES

● Once you've answered the 3 W's and decided on the structure of your presentation, you'll want to start making notes. But, however carefully you prepare yourself, experience has shown that, if you're like most speakers, you'll abandon your voluminous notes as soon as you hit the platform and rely on wordy, boring overhead transparencies. People like Tony Buzan have shown that **KEYWORDS** are all your brain needs to trigger back all the information you've prepared and that **DRAWINGS** and **LOGOS** are even more effective for recall. You'll find that condensing your notes onto one **A6 CARD** like the example shown overleaf is quite sufficient as a memory aid - and it leaves you free to use bold and simple transparencies, slides and flip-charts.

⑦

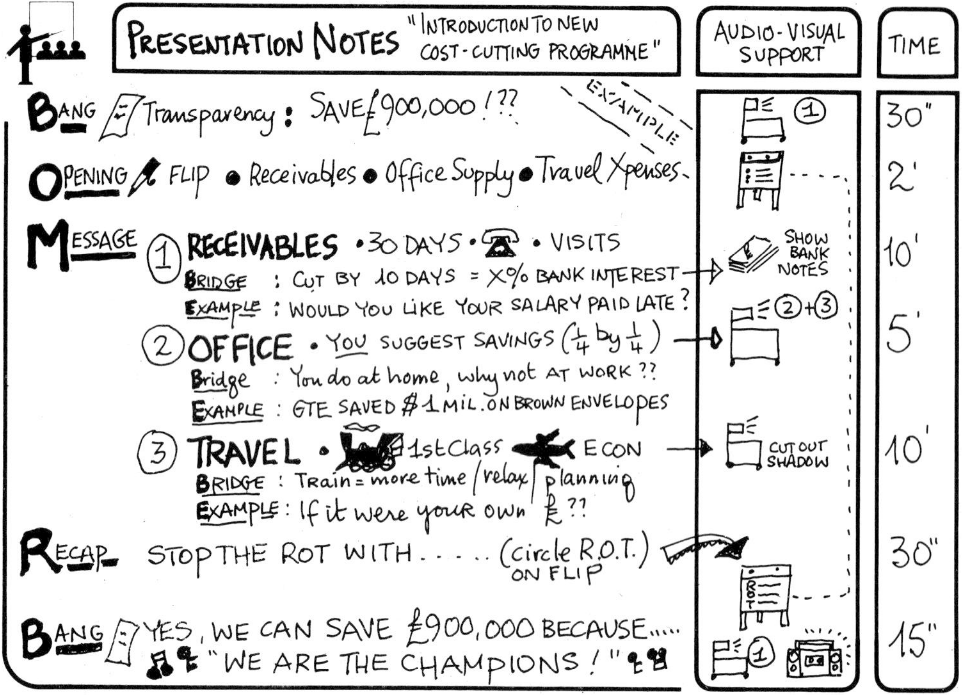
PRESENTATION NOTES
"INTRODUCTION TO NEW COST-CUTTING PROGRAMME"
AUDIO-VISUAL SUPPORT
TIME
EXAMPLE
BANG
Transparency: SAVE £900,000 !??
30"
OPENING
FLIP • Receivables • Office Supply • Travel Xpenses.
2'
MESSAGE
1 RECEIVABLES • 30 DAYS • • VISITS
BRIDGE : CUT BY 10 DAYS = X% BANK INTEREST
EXAMPLE : WOULD YOU LIKE YOUR SALARY PAID LATE?
SHOW BANK NOTES
10'
2 OFFICE • YOU SUGGEST SAVINGS (¼ by ¼)
Bridge : You do at home, why not AT WORK ??
EXAMPLE : GTE SAVED $1 MIL. ON BROWN ENVELOPES
2 + 3
5'
3 TRAVEL • 1st Class ECON
BRIDGE : Train = more time / relax / planning
EXAMPLE : If it were your own £ ??
CUT OUT SHADOW
10'
RECAP
STOP THE ROT WITH ..... (circle R.O.T.) ON FLIP
R O T
30"
BANG
YES, WE CAN SAVE £900,000 BECAUSE.....
"WE ARE THE CHAMPIONS!"
15"

2. MAKING YOUR PRESENTATION

MAKING YOUR PRESENTATION
THE OPENING BANG

Your audience has almost always something better to do with their minds than to listen to you. In order to show respect and make them **want** to hear you out............

ALWAYS START WITH A *Bang !*

- A provocative or dramatic statement

- A humorous anecdote (not a joke - it's sure to offend **someone** in the audience !)

- Audience participation (a question, a survey of views, a reference to participants etc.)

- An audio-visual "gimmick" (slide, video, tape etc.)

- An object (a "prop", a product, a model etc.)

- An action (a demonstration, a mime, an unexpected entry, a song, a quotation, other "actors" etc.)

Business Presentations

MAKING YOUR PRESENTATION
THE FINAL BANG

Most business presentations end with mumbled requests for questions, apologies or other whimpers. Do yourself a favour and.............

ALWAYS FINISH WITH A
Bang!

- A statement which dramatically sums up your key message

- A visual or verbal link back to your opening bang

- An unexpected action, happening or apparition

- Simply a determined "Thankyou for your attention" (always "ask" for applause even if you won't get it)

Imagine..... that each presentation is a gift for the audience. If the "vehicle" and the structure are the wrapping the ending bang is the ribbon !

Business Presentations

NERVES: THE MURPHY MONKEY

As you get up to speak, it's as if a monkey has suddenly jumped onto your shoulders. He claws your neck and weighs you down - making your knees feel weak and shaky. As you start to speak, he pulls at your vocal chords and dries up your saliva. He pushes your eyes to the floor, makes your arms feel 10 metres long and attaches a piece of elastic to your belt - pulling you back to the table or wall behind you !

Experienced speakers know about the Murphy monkey. Within the first 30 seconds they throw him to the audience ! When you throw the monkey to one of the participants, suddenly the spotlight is on them and not on you. How...?

● A question, a show of hands, a short "icebreaker" (participant introductions, an exercise or quiz etc.) a discussion, a "volunteer" or simply a reference to one or more of the participants - all these are ways of putting the monkey on **their** backs for a few moments.

This takes the pressure off you and gives you time to relax, smile and get ready to communicate your message loud and clear.

USING YOUR VOICE

P ROJECTION — Speak louder than usual. Throw your voice to back of room

A RTICULATION — Don't swallow words.
Beware of verbal "tics"

M ODULATION — Vary tone and pitch. Be dramatic, confidential and/or triumphant

P RONUNCIATION — Watch tonic accents. Check difficult words. Beware of malapropisms

E NUNCIATION — Over emphasize.
Accentuate syllables

R EPETITION — Repeat key phrases with different vocal emphasis

S PEED — Use delivery speed to manipulate the audience! Fast delivery to excite and stimulate. Slow delivery to emphasize, awe, dramatize and control.

(13)

Business Presentations

MAKING YOUR PRESENTATION
DRESS

- Avoid black and white and other strongly contrasting colours

- Wear comfortable, loose-fitting clothes

- If you can't make up your mind, wear something boring - at least your clothes won't detract from the message !

- Try and dress one step above the audience

- Check zips and buttons before standing up

When in doubt, a blue blazer, grey slacks and black shoes with a white shirt and striped tie is usually acceptable from the board room to the art studio.

Business Presentations

MAKING YOUR PRESENTATION
PLATFORM SKILLS
TEN TIPS

> The day I lose my stage-fright is the day I stop acting
> Sir Laurence Olivier

❏ Don't keep your eyes on your notes

❏ Never read anything except quotations

❏ If you're not nervous there's something wrong

❏ Exaggerate body movements and verbal emphasis

❏ **PERFORM** (don't act) Perform = "fournir" (to supply) and "per" (for)

❏ Pause often - silence is much longer for **you** than for the audience

❏ Use humour. A laugh is worth a thousand frowns !

❏ Be enthusiastic. If you're not, why should they be ?

❏ Don't try and win the Nobel prize for technical accuracy

❏ **KISS**. **K**eep **I**t **S**imple, **S**tupid !

LIGHTHOUSE TECHNIQUE

Sweep the audience with your eyes, staying only 2-3 seconds on each person - unless in dialogue. This will give each participant the impression that you are speaking to him/her personally and ensure attention, in the same way as the lighthouse keeps you awake by its regular sweeping flash of light. Above all, avoid looking at one (friendly-looking) member of the audience or at a fixed (non-threatening) point on the wall or floor.

TIMING

Remember the 50% rule.
Rehearse it. Time it. Cut it by 50%. This will ensure that you allow for • late start • over-run by previous speaker • sharing passing thoughts triggered by the environment • participants' questions etc.

Always stick to the schedule - whatever the consequences. Over-running on a presentation is **always** bad because:

● the senior participants will conclude that you can't plan and worry about the schedule - and your career !

● your fellow speakers will resent you taking **their** time

● non-speaking participants will stop listening and start thinking about coffee or lunch or their holiday in Spain

(17)

MANNERISMS

- Don't be tempted by manual props (pens, pointers, spectacles etc.)
- Don't keep loose change in your pocket
- Be aware of your verbal tics and work on eliminating them (i.e. "OK!" — "You know" — "and so forth" — "Now ...")
- Don't smoke (unless seated in discussion mode)
- Watch out for furniture!
- Avoid "closed" or tense body positions
- Don't worry about pacing, leaning etc.
- Check your hair/tie/trousers/dress before standing up!

DISCUSSION LEADING

Take a tip from the Ancient Greeks.

If you wish to encourage audience participation to prove a point use SOCRATIC DIRECTION

K now the answers you want

O pen questioning technique

P araphrase participants' answers

S ummarize contributions (flip chart?)

A dd your own points

QUESTIONS & INTERRUPTIONS

Most participant questions are not questions.
They are requests for the spotlight. If it's one of those rare, closed REAL questions — answer it succinctly.
If not, first:

●  back to the questioner what you thought was the question. ("If I understand correctly, you're asking ....")

Depending on how the questioner "reformulates" the question, answer it OR:

●  it as follows:

- **GROUP** : "How do the rest of the group feel?"
  : "Has anyone else had a similar problem?"
- **RICOCHET** : (to one participant) "Bill, you're an expert on this?"
- **REVERSE** : (back to questioner) "You've obviously done some thinking on this. What's **your** view?"

Business Presentations

DEALING WITH DIFFICULT PARTICIPANTS

1. THE HECKLER:

- Probably insecure
- Gets satisfaction from needling
- Aggressive and argumentative

What to do:

- Never get upset
- Find merit, express agreement, move on
- Wait for a mis-statement fact and then throw it out to the group for correction

DEALING WITH DIFFICULT PARTICIPANTS

2. THE TALKER/KNOW ALL
- An "eager beaver"/chatterbox
- A show-off
- Well-informed and anxious to show it

What to do:

- Wait 'til he/she take a breath, thank, refocus and move on
- Slow him/her down with a tough question
- Jump in and ask for group to comment

DEALING WITH DIFFICULT PARTICIPANTS

3. THE GRIPER

- Feels "hard done by"
- Probably has a pet "peeve"
- Will use you as scapegoat

What to do:

- Get him/her to be specific
- Show that the purpose of your presentation is to be positive and constructive
- Use peer pressure

DEALING WITH DIFFICULT PARTICIPANTS

4. THE WHISPERERS
    (There's only one.
    The other is the
    "whisperee"!)

- Don't understand what's going on
  — clarifying or translating
- Sharing anecdotes triggered by
  your presentation
- Bored, mischievous or hypo-
  critical (unusual)

What to do:

- Stop talking, wait for them to look up and "non-verbally" ask for
  their permission to continue

- Use "lighthouse" technique

DEALING WITH DIFFICULT PARTICIPANTS

5. THE "WRONG" ONE

- Has the facts wrong or ...
- Is just plain stupid!
- Is confused or incoherent in verbal expression

What to do:

- Wrong? Thank and ask for group comment (Let the group correct)
- Confused/Incoherent? Say, "let me see if I have understood what you mean" Then tactfully restate.

SUMMARY: 10 GOLDEN RULES FOR PUBLIC SPEAKING

1   Take 3 deep breaths before starting
2   Always start with a bang!!!
3   Always get SOME Audience participation right from the start
4   Tell'em what you're gonna tell'em; Tell'em; Tell'em what you told'em
5   Never read anything except quotations
6   Be a lighthouse!
7   Use PAMPERS (Projection, Articulation, Modulation, Pronounciation, Enunciation, Repetition, Speed)
8   Watch your Mannerisms!
9   Always stick to schedule
10 Always end with a bang — not with a whimper

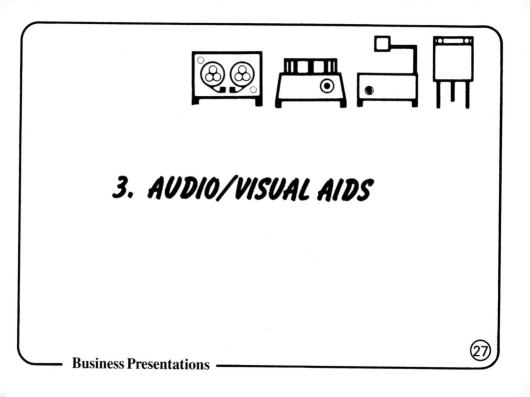

3. AUDIO/VISUAL AIDS

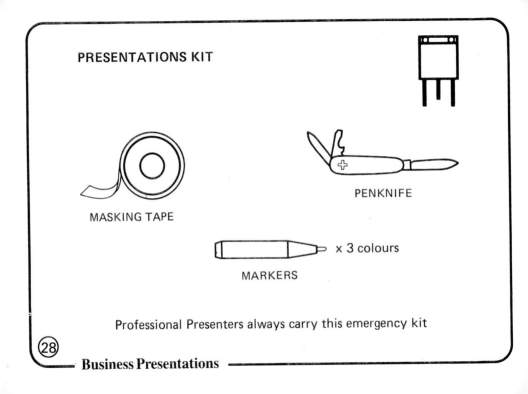

FLIP CHART RULES

- Make sure you have enough paper and a spare block/roll

- Check that there are several THICK, WORKING, COLOURED markers (i.e. Always bring your own!)

- Check flip chart stand for stability

PREPARATION

INVISIBLE OUTLINE

Lightly pencil in headings in advance when unsured of space drawing, handwriting etc.

CORNER CRIB

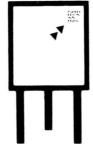

Use the top corner to pencil in your notes for each chart. Write small and no one will notice!

READY-MADE

Prepare key charts in advance

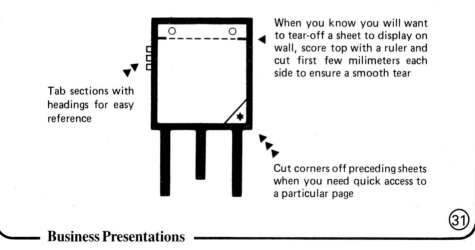

FLIP TIPS
PAPER

When you know you will want to tear-off a sheet to display on wall, score top with a ruler and cut first few milimeters each side to ensure a smooth tear

Tab sections with headings for easy reference

Cut corners off preceding sheets when you need quick access to a particular page

GRAPHICS

TTRACTIVE

- Give each flip a title
- Use bullet points (like on this page)
- Use at least 2 dark colours

BIG & BOLD

- Use THICK markers (bring your own!)
- Should be legible from 10 metres!

CAPITAL KEYWORDS

- Never write sentences!

Business Presentations

FLIP TIPS

GRAPHICS

Whenever possible use cartoons or drawings to personalize and add interest to your headings

$ 1 MILLION

7 SENIOR MANAGERS

3 PLANTS

SOCRATIC DIRECTION

(33)

Business Presentations

GRAPHICS

STANDING

Every time you turn your back on the audience your voice and their attention disappear.

Stand like the person in this diagram and try and face the audience while you write.

If you find it too uncomfortable make sure you don't talk **while** you write.

Stand by the side of the chart, talk, write and talk again.

O/H PROJECTOR RULES

THE PROJECTOR

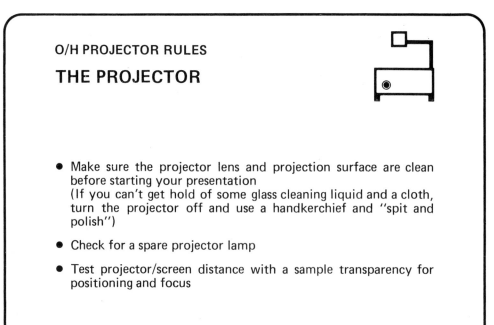

- Make sure the projector lens and projection surface are clean before starting your presentation
  (If you can't get hold of some glass cleaning liquid and a cloth, turn the projector off and use a handkerchief and "spit and polish")

- Check for a spare projector lamp

- Test projector/screen distance with a sample transparency for positioning and focus

Business Presentations

SCREEN POSITION

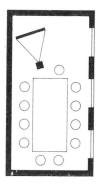

- The best position for the screen is in a corner of the conference room — high enough for everyone to see without craning, peeping, standing or !eaning!

Business Presentations

O/H PROJECTOR RULES

PROJECTION ANGLE

- Avoiding the "Keystone" effect

Keep the projector beam at 90° to the screen by tilting the screen (ideal) or by jacking up the projector until keystone disappears. If you jack the projector you'll need a chock to prevent transparencies sliding forward.

PROJECTOR POSITIONING

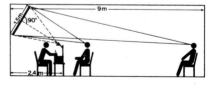

Business Presentations

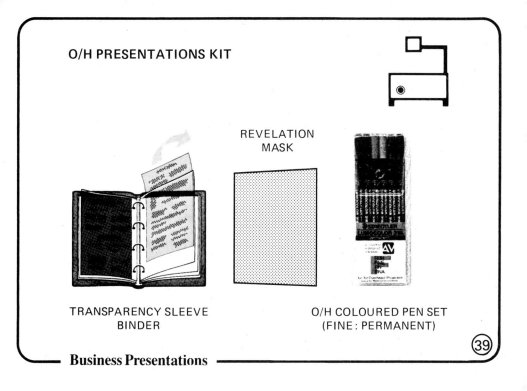

O/H PRESENTATIONS KIT

REVELATION MASK

TRANSPARENCY SLEEVE BINDER

O/H COLOURED PEN SET (FINE: PERMANENT)

(39)

Business Presentations

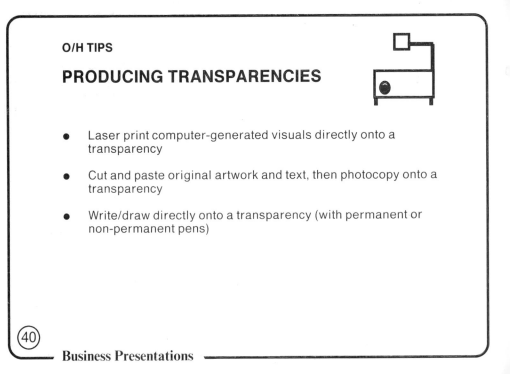

O/H TIPS

PRODUCING TRANSPARENCIES

- Laser print computer-generated visuals directly onto a transparency

- Cut and paste original artwork and text, then photocopy onto a transparency

- Write/draw directly onto a transparency (with permanent or non-permanent pens)

Business Presentations

PLANNING A PRESENTATION

USE THE "STORYBOARD" APPROACH

- One transparency with **chapter headings**

- One transparency **per** chapter heading

- One transparency per point/topic in each chapter

TIPS

- Use consistent design (see p. 42)

- Print series name & number on each

- Concentrate message in centre

- Use only $\frac{2}{3}$ of space for message

(41)

GOLDEN RULES

FRAME — Use a standard, HORIZONTAL frame & "logo" (like this page!) for all transparencies

LARGE — USE LARGE LEGIBLE LETTERS
Titles: 1-2 cm. Text 0.5-1 cm.

IMAGES — Use at least one IMAGE or IKON on every transparency

COLOUR — Use at least one colour other than black on every transparency

KISS — **K**ey words only   **S**ix lines max.
1 topic per transparency   **S**ix words per line max

Business Presentations

LETTERING

Computer generated

- Use Helvetica Bold for titles & Times for text

Handwritten (onto final transparency)

- Use permanent O/H pens
- Place transparency on squared paper to ensure alignment
- Use colour as much as possible
- Be bold! Practise your own "alphabet"
- For full letters, use light colour to block in letters before outlining with darker colour

ABCDEFGHIJKLMNOPQRSTUVWXYZ!?

(43)

SYMBOLS

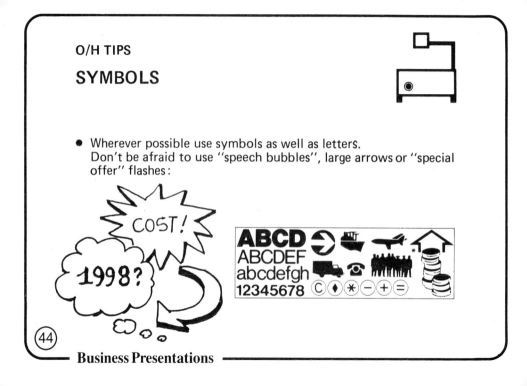

- Wherever possible use symbols as well as letters.
  Don't be afraid to use "speech bubbles", large arrows or "special
  offer" flashes:

Business Presentations

GRAPHICS

Always try and avoid showing columns of figures:

- Design graphs, charts or tables using several colours
- Make lines bold – even if less accurate
- Reduce numbers and letters to minimum
- Use overlay technique for superimposed graphs
- Keep pie-chart numbers horizontal

N.B. Whenever you employ a graphic artist to design your transparencies (whether on a computer or manually) ALWAYS give clear instructions and ALWAYS ask for a draft or a model before committing yourself.

(45)

Business Presentations

PRESENTATION TECHNIQUES

WITH PLASTIC FRAME (Staedler)

OVERLAY

- Use several superimposed transparencies to build up a story or argument

  NB Make sure you mount your overlays so that they fit onto each other exactly — everytime

WITH CARD FRAME (3M)

Business Presentations

PRESENTATION TECHNIQUES

REVELATION

◀ • When you have several important points on one transparency, use a mask to gradually reveal your argument step by step.
(If you don't, your audience will be reading point 6 when you're talking about point 1)

◀ • For important, high quality presentation, try the "window" technique

(47)

Business Presentations

PRESENTATION TECHNIQUES

ANIMATION

- Solid objects or cut-outs on the projection surface will block the light and give sharp silhouettes on the screen
  With cardboard cut-outs you can design an interesting and original animated presentation

EXAMPLE:

Production process, moving arrow.
Female silhouette, light bulb etc.

SPECIAL TIP ▶ Could be a good opening BANG!

Business Presentations

PRESENTATION TECHNIQUES

- Use a POINTER to highlight messages

    eg: cut out arrow, transparent pointing finger, pen or pencil (be careful it doesn't roll off) or a laser pointer.

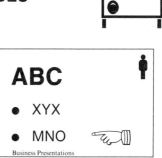

- Place pointer on the transparency and move as you change messages. **DON'T HOLD IT**. Murphy says your hand will shake!

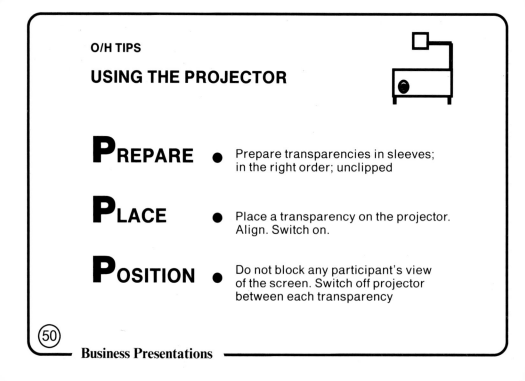

O/H TIPS

USING THE PROJECTOR

PREPARE • Prepare transparencies in sleeves; in the right order; unclipped

PLACE • Place a transparency on the projector. Align. Switch on.

POSITION • Do not block any participant's view of the screen. Switch off projector between each transparency

WHEN TO USE PHOTOGRAPHIC SLIDES?

- When you have the time and the money!

- When you need a "higher quality" presentation

- When you want to show photographs/cartoons etc.

- When you wish to change pace or differentiate from colleagues' omnipresent overhead slides

- When you wish to dramatize a point and create expectancy by darkening the conference room

- When contact with and participation of the audience is not essential

(51)

WHEN NOT TO USE PHOTOGRAPHIC SLIDES

- When you only have words to show
- When you can't darken the room sufficiently
- When audience participation is important
- When you are a persuasive "eye contact" speaker
- When you have a tight budget!
- When "everybody else does, so I suppose ..."
- When you don't know how to work the projector

PHOTOGRAPHIC SLIDES
THE MISSING LINK

Many slide presentations fail because they forget that slides should be used as VISUALS. Examples of where slides can be used to clarify things visually are:

- Charts and Graphs — instead of tables

- Diagrams of processes — instead of words

- Photographs — instead of descriptions

- Flow charts — instead of lists

- Graphic Titles (Logos, Drawings etc.)

- Cartoons — instead of anecdotes

SLIDE RULES

Make sure the agency/friend who does your slides will:

- Always use several colours
- Be aware and beware of "colour camouflage" (i.e. no yellow on white, blue on green, pink on red etc.)
- Never put more than 6 lines of max. 6 words (Ideal = what you could write on a T-shirt)
- Use photos, cartoons, drawings as much as possible
- Use a consistent design for series of slides
- Keep words horizontal (especially on pie charts)
- Never show photos of pages from a book
- Remember that words are not visual aids!

PHOTOGRAPHIC SLIDES
SLIDE-PROJECTOR/TAPE LINK UP

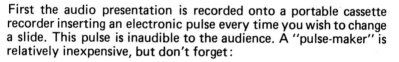

First the audio presentation is recorded onto a portable cassette recorder inserting an electronic pulse every time you wish to change a slide. This pulse is inaudible to the audience. A ''pulse-maker'' is relatively inexpensive, but don't forget:

- Not everyone is an expert in recording this kind of voice-over. You need special skill

- For a previously recorded message to come over loud and clear you need a good amplifier and speakers (heavy, costly, subject to Murphy's law!)

SLIDE PRESENTATION RULES

- Check the projector lamp before going on
- Mark each slide for correct insertion in the carousel
- Do a dry run to check that slides are in the right order and the right way up and round
- Stand away from projector — use remote control
- Use "black" slides for natural breaks
- Explain what is on the screen — but don't read text
- If you have to talk too — double your enthusiasm and use PAMPERS!

MULTI-PROJECTOR ANIMATION

This is a highly complex and delicate approach to slide projection which should be made only by real professionals.

The combination of tape recording and several projectors means that you can superimpose images and accomplish fade outs and/or flashing, mobile figures on the screen to a spoken and/or musical background.

This process is effectively used in customer presentations of products or processes but is very fragile.

The necessary synchronization of all the various elements lends itself to Murphy's law (If something can go wrong, it will!)

THE CASSETTE RECORDER/PLAYER
MUSIC

Here are some ways you could use recorded music to liven up a presentation:

- As a "sound track" to a slide presentation
- As an introduction as you walk to the podium
- As background music during coffee breaks/intervals
- Snatches or verses of songs to illustrate a point amusingly

  - EXAMPLE:

    Customer Service Presentation: "Help", "You can't always get what you want", "Satisfaction", "Keep the customer satisfied", "I need you"

THE CASSETTE RECORDER/PLAYER
VOICE

Recorded speech can be useful for:

- Illustrating role-plays (Interviewing, Public Speaking, Sales-man-Customer, Boss-Subordinate)

- Examples of opinions (market research interviews etc.)

- Bringing an absent colleague to the conference!

- Interjecting humorous anecdotes

- Giving examples of current radio ads/trends

Business Presentations

RECORDING

- Use a cassette deck to record your presentation so you can work on your mistakes

- Record a colleague's presentation and edit it for use in meetings with subordinates

  NB When recording audio examples make sure you leave very little space between each recording. In this way you can press the "pause" button at the end of one example knowing that the next recording is cued to start as soon as you next hit the button

VHF COMMUNICATION

Human beings store incoming data in one of 3 ways:

Visual: they memorize pictures, images, diagrams, charts, graphics, etc.

Hearing: they memorize sounds, conversations, melodies, accents, etc.

Feeling: they memorize emotions, smells, tastes, tactile experiences and ... pain

However, each of us has a preferred "channel" for remembering data (V, H or F). So, the good speaker provides his varied audience with as wide a range of stimuli as possible. Here's a resumé of the aids and techniques available to you:

Visual Aids
● Flip Chart ● White/Metaplan (Pin) Board ● Overhead Projector ● Slide Projector ● Props ● Video Clips ● Word Pictures

Hearing Aids
● Audio Cassettes ● Video ● Sound Effects ● Music ● Onomatopoeia

Feeling Aids
● Music ● Handouts ● Props ● Anecdotes, Analogies and Parables ● Discussions & Exercises
Remember: feelings stay longer than facts

⑥²

Business Presentations

CHECKLIST

4. PRESENTATION CHECKLIST

DISPROVING MURPHY'S LAW

CHECKLIST

"If something can go wrong — it will!
  or, as Robert Burns said:
"The best laid schemes o' mice an' men gang aft aglae"

- In order to try and disprove Murphy's law next time you have to make a presentation, make sure you:

  - Use a Presentation Checklist
  - Go to the conference room the day before the presentation and go through your checklist. Make sure you talk to someone responsible about missing items
  - Go to the conference room again at least 30 minutes before the start of the morning/afternoon session when you are on and go through everything once again.
    If it's good enough for Swissair, it's good enough for you!

PRESENTATION CHECKLIST

	①✓	②✓	NOTES
PRESENTATION			
Presentation Cards			
Overheads			
Slides			
Cassettes (Video/Audio)			
Handouts			
Gimmicks			
ACCESSORIES			
Pointer			
Felt Tip Markers			
Overhead Pens			
Masking Tape			
Pen Knife			
Spare Flip Chart			
Plugs/Extensions			
A/V EQUIPMENT			
Flip Chart Stand			
Blackboard/White			
Overhead Projector			
• Spare Lamp ?			
Screen (Tilted)			
Carousel Projector			
• Spare Lamp ?			
• Spare Cartridge ?			
• Remote Control (Ext. ?)			
Cassette Recorder			
Video Equipment			
Amplifier/Speakers			
Microphone			

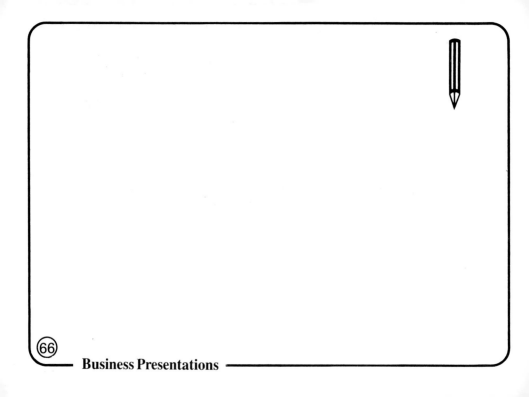

Business Presentations

5. *TELEVISION INTERVIEWS*

TELEVISION INTERVIEWS

MURPHY'S LAW OF VIDEO EDITING

When deciding which extract to choose from your recorded interview, speech or press conference the editor will always go for the bit which:

- you liked the least

- shows you saying something controversial
  (and leave out any qualification, explanation or proviso you made)

- supports an argument which the presenter wants to make —
  regardless of the context in which you spoke

WHAT YOU SAY

THE 3 "A'S"

- **ADVANTAGES** — Whatever the question or context, stress the advantages of what you're saying/selling for Mr/Ms Everyperson

- **APPLICATIONS** — Wherever possible turn complicated questions/answers into examples of applications of what you're saying/selling to the lives of Mr/Ms Everyperson

- **ANALOGIES** — Everytime you feel that the interviewer is leading you into technical explanations, try and think of simple analogies to illustrate your point

WHAT YOU SAY

THE K.I.S.S. PRINCIPLE

Whenever in doubt **K**eep **I**t **S**imple **S**tupid !

- Very few TV programmes are aimed at people who are experts in your field. Even if they tell you that it's for a specialised documentary, the chances are that the "clip" will be used in a programme with mass audience appeal

SO   Aim your remarks at the man/woman in the street — without being patronizing and without distorting facts

WHAT YOU SAY

DON'T KNOCK COMPETITION

Avoid making any comments on the weakness of your competitors (unless you're a politician, in which case this is the **only** thing you'll be able to talk about!) Remain non-committal especially with "what if ... ?" questions.

No names — no pack drill !

WHAT YOU SAY

AVOID MAKING "GOOD T.V."

Remember the man who hit Bernard Levin in the 60's or the fight on Dutch T.V. in 1984? Any example of live controversy will be sold to T.V. companies around the world and **always** to your detriment. In fact interviewers who are hard up for action sometimes attempt to provoke aggressiveness in their questions and behaviour.

Don't be bland but avoid making "saleable" television

TELEVISION INTERVIEWS
HOW YOU SAY IT

NERVES

If you're not nervous then there's something wrong !

- Breath deeply and slowly several times before the cameras go live
- Keep some water handy for a dry mouth
- Smile as often as possible. You can't overdo it
- Keep your body language "open" even when you think you're off camera
  - never cross/fold your arms
  - use open/upward palm gestures
  - keep hands, glasses, pen etc. away from mouth

HOW TO ANSWER DIFFICULT QUESTIONS

THE TWO-SEATER HELICOPTER TECHNIQUE

Sometimes an interviewer will surprise you by prefacing a question with a value judgement with which you disagree. ("Some people have suggested ..." "it seems to me that ...")

- Smile before you reply
- Get up in a two-seater helicopter and look down at the "problem" as if you were beside the interviewer
- Say something like: "if you look at it that way, I can understand that it seems ... but if you look at another way, then ..."

HOW TO ANSWER DIFFICULT QUESTIONS

REFRAMING

Interviewers will often "frame" their questions in a negative way. To reframe successfully you:

- Give a "receipt" to the interviewer for the question i.e. "Yes, some people have taken that view recently" or "I can understand why you see things in this way ..."

- Change the framework or context of the question by continuing ... "but have you ever thought that this means ..." or "I wonder if people realize that this is because ..."

HOW TO ANSWER DIFFICULT QUESTIONS

ONE STEP BEYOND

With trick questions that try and catch you out on an inconsistency or seeming contradiction in statements, actions or policy:

- acknowledge the negative bias in the question and then go one step further — towards **your** answer.

    Example   "Yes, that's true and I'd like to emphasize that this is the very reason for our/my insistence on .... in our/my new programme/action/statement."

6. *PRESS CONFERENCES*

MURPHY'S PRESS RELEASE LAW

However watertight and "comfortable" your press release sounds to you, at least one of the journalists will take pleasure in needling you on unrelated issues.

O'Connor's Corrolary

None of the journalists will stick to the script

JOURNALISTS

Most journalists are terrible questioners in that they are much more concerned with showing you and the other journalists what **they** know than with asking you what **you** think !

PRESS CONFERENCES

GAINING TIME

You will have more time to "gain time" in a press conference than in a live or recorded TV interview. Whenever you are faced with a question that needs some care, here are some techniques:

- Repeat the question by paraphrasing what you feel to be the key (and most advantageous) element to **you**
- Smile and say, "before I answer that specific question I need to explain some of the background ..."
- Deflect the question to a colleague stating why you are deflecting it — thus giving him/her an opportunity to gather their thoughts
- Take a few moments to discuss the PREMISE of the question rather than the answer. Example: "You mentioned that more and more people are worried about ... In fact a recent survey showed that, on the contrary, people ..."
- Ask the journalist to be more specific with the question

GAINING EMPATHY

2. Techniques

- Be relaxed and be yourself
- Smile as often as possible
- Never say "no comment" but explain **why** it is inappropriate for you to comment
- Don't be afraid to say "I don't know"
- Avoid sarcasm :
  Don't say "Unfortunately, Mr Journalist I have decided to leave my crystal ball in the offices of your esteemed newspaper where I feel it will be used much more often than in our more down-to-earth policy meetings"
- Don't be obsequious or use flattery — journalists are impervious to it
- Never say "I'm glad you asked that question" It's the number one no-no with hard-bitten, road-weary journalists

GAINING EMPATHY

1. General

A very general rule that we have discovered about human relation-ships is that people like people who are not infallible. A major element in interpersonal attraction is the élan of tenderness we feel for open admissions of inadequacy.

Although the press conference is **NOT** to be seen as an official forum for the sharing of feelings of incompetence, no person should think that s/he has to have **THE** answer to every twisted, convolluted question about complex figures, social implications of policy or philosophical considerations of second level abstraction.

PRESS CONFERENCES

GAINING CONTROL

In order to control a press conference you must constantly put yourself in the journalists' shoes and ask ... "if I were representing a newspaper ...

- What facts **must** I have in order to construct some kind of story?
- What facts would I **like** to have to make the story more sensational?
- What negative information could help me show the readers both sides of the argument?
- What seemingly unrelated issues/points could I use to colour my main argument (either for or against)?

This mental empathy will lead you to EXPECT unpleasant questions and prepare you to counter them with your positive messages.

PRESS CONFERENCES

REMEMBER!

- You can't convince all of the people all of the time

- People only really hear what they want to hear

- You are proud of what you and/or your organization are doing

FEEDBACK

7. FEEDBACK

CONSTRUCTIVE CRITIQUE OF PRESENTATIONS

FEEDBACK

- EMPHASIZE GOOD POINTS
- SAY "YOU": ADDRESS REMARKS TO SPEAKER
- CRITIQUE CONSTRUCTIVELY: OFFER ALTERNATIVES

EXAMPLES

- "I think it would have been more effective if you had ..."
- "I'd have been very interested in hearing more about ..."
- If we were in a larger room I think people at the back might have difficulty hearing some parts of your presentation

Business Presentations

FEEDBACK CARD

NAME

SPEECH

		NEEDS IMPROVEMENT ✓
WHY?	• Was the objective of the presentation clear?	
	• Had the speaker analyzed why he was speaking?	
WHO?	• Did the audience know what to do or think at the end?	
	• Did the speaker pitch speech to audience level?	
	• Were the audience interested?	
	• Did audience resent any remarks?	
WHAT?	BANG	
	OPENING	
	MESSAGE — BRIDGE? EXAMPLES?	
	RECAP	
	BANG	
HOW?	VOICE	
	SPEED	
	POSTURE	
	EYE CONTACT	
	MANNERISMS	
	HUMOUR	
	GIMMICKS	
	VOCABULARY	
	TIMING	
	AUDIO-VISUAL AIDS: FLIP CHART — O/H — SLIDES — TAPE — PROPS	

(87)

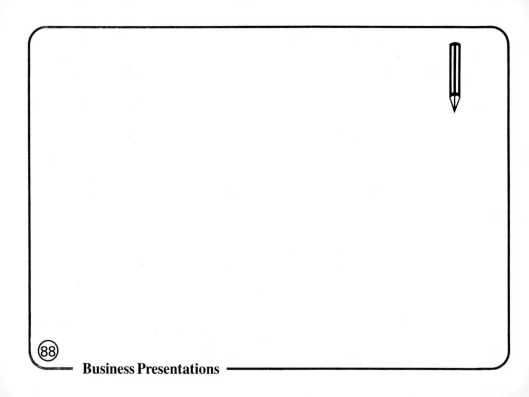

Business Presentations

MASTERS

8. MASTERS FOR REPRODUCTION

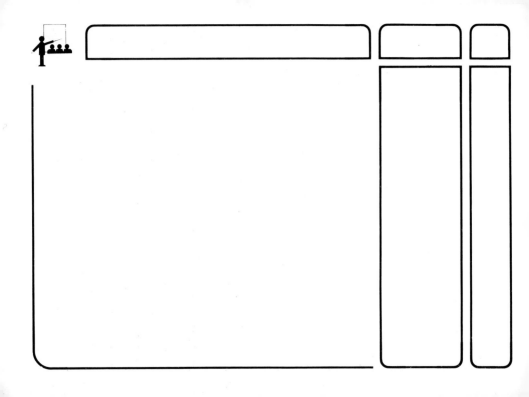

PRESENTATION CHECKLIST

	①✓	②✓	NOTES
PRESENTATION			
Presentation Cards			
Overheads			
Slides			
Cassettes (Video/Audio)			
Handouts			
Gimmicks			
ACCESSORIES			
Pointer			
Felt Tip Markers			
Overhead Pens			
Masking Tape			
Pen Knife			
Spare Flip Chart			
Plugs/Extensions			
A/V EQUIPMENT			
Flip Chart Stand			
Blackboard/White			
Overhead Projector			
• Spare Lamp?			
Screen (Tilted)			
Carousel Projector			
• Spare Lamp?			
• Spare Cartridge?			
• Remote Control (Ext.?)			
Cassette Recorder			
Video Equipment			
Amplifier/Speakers			
Microphone			

FEEDBACK CARD

NAME _____

SPEECH _____

		✓	NEEDS IMPROVEMENT
WHY?	• Was the objective of the presentation clear?		
	• Had the speaker analyzed why he was speaking?		
WHO?	• Did the audience know what to do or think at the end?		
	• Did the speaker pitch speech to audience level?		
	• Were the audience interested?		
	• Did audience resent any remarks?		
WHAT?	BANG		
	OPENING		
	MESSAGE — BRIDGE? EXAMPLES?		
	RECAP		
	BANG		
HOW?	VOICE		
	SPEED		
	POSTURE		
	EYE CONTACT		
	MANNERISMS		
	HUMOUR		
	GIMMICKS		
	VOCABULARY		
	TIMING		
	AUDIO-VISUAL AIDS: FLIP CHART, O/H, SLIDES, TAPE, PROPS		

About the Author

John Townsend BA MA MIPD is Managing Director of Interaction Training Seminars and Workshops. He founded Interaction (which is a member of Team Training International) after 20 years of experience in international human resource management positions in the UK, France, the United States and Switzerland. From 1978-1984 he was European Director of Executive Development with GTE in Geneva with training responsibility for over 800 managers in some 15 countries. Mr Townsend has published a number of management and professional guides, including the very popular 'Instructor's Pocketbook', and regularly contributes articles to leading management and training journals. In addition to teaching a range of specialised management and training skills seminars to multi-national clients, he is also a regular speaker at conferences and briefings throughout Europe.

Interaction, Training Seminars and Workshops,
Rue de Bejou, Ornex 01210 Ferney-Voltaire, France.

Published by :-
Management Pocketbooks Ltd

All rights reserved

© COPYRIGHT JOHN TOWNSEND 1985, 1993
EDITIONS: 1st 1985, 5th 1993. Reprinted 1995

PRINTED IN ENGLAND BY ALRESFORD PRESS LTD, ALRESFORD, HANTS.   ISBN 1870471 180

ORDER FORM

Please send me .... copies of   'The Business Presenter's Pocketbook'

.... copies of   ....Pocketbook

.... copies of   ....Pocketbook

.... copies of   ....Pocketbook

.... copies of   ....Pocketbook

Name .... Position ....

Company ....

Address ....

....

....

....

Telephone .... Telex/Fax ....

VAT No. (EC companies) ....Your Order Ref ....

Management Pocketbooks Ltd
14 East Street, Alresford
Hampshire SO24 9EE
Tel: (01962) 735573
Fax: (01962) 733637